OUT OF THE WILDERNESS: INTO THE PROMISE

THE JOURNEY AND DEVOTIONAL
OF VICTORY OVER CANCER

PAMELA HARDING

In Appreciation

I want to thank first of all, My Lord and Savior, Jesus Christ for giving me life.

My wonderful husband, John, who has never stood in the way of my relationship with God, and who has always stood by my side, and always will, through it all.

Acknowledging the Spiritual Generals in my life, Apostle Don Lyon, Apostle Jonathan Byrd, Pastor Felix Okoroji, a very special thank you to each of you. You are who I've asked God to place before me to show me how deep I am able to go in Christ.

Pastor Miriam Williams and Apostle Jonathan Byrd for their guidance in this publication.

And a very special thank you to my baby sister, Lori Erecius, who painstakingly took the time to put up with me, again, to edit this book. Just another day in the life of her big sister....

Table of Contents

Foreword by Apostle Don Lyon

If you wonder why you face problems, read this book!

If you wonder why your prayers didn't get answered, read this book!

If you don't' understand your circumstances, read this book!

If your church confuses you, read this book!

If someone anointed you and no change comes, read this book!

If you prayed, fasted and nothing happened, read this book!

You will find more answers to your questions in this book than most places you search! I recommend this book to new believers and to those who have known God for years!

Pastor Pam has proven the principles she writes about from years of experience. The results are of her testimony of several healings and miracles.

If you have a friend who is struggling in their walk with God, you would do them a great favor if you give them this book. I strongly endorse it!

Apostle Don Lyon, D.D.

Foreword by Apostle Jonathan Byrd

The author reveals that dynamite comes in small packages. *Out of the Wilderness: Into the Promise* by Pastor Pamela Harding, is a testimony filled with the grace of God to transform and heal a life that was broken beyond her repair. Her life was full of deadly challenges that almost destroyed her and her marriage. Standing at death's door, having been diagnosed with stage three cancer, she turned to Jesus, the author and finisher of faith, refusing to be shaken by a report of death, believing that Jesus came and brought healing and deliverance for her. A covenant promise that transformed into the power of God.

This is a captivating testimony that will build ever increasing faith in your heart to stand on His promises. "What the Savior did for Pam, He'll do the same for you."

Ephesians 6:13 says, *'Therefore take up the whole armor of God, that you may be able to withstand in the evil day, and having done all, to* ***STAND!***

Apostle Jonathan Byrd

Synopsis

Having been diagnosed with 3rd stage lung cancer that had gone into the lymph nodes, Pamela Harding, being a Christian, had a choice to make, believe the doctor's report and die, or to stand on God's Word and receive the Report of The Lord.

Out of the Wilderness reveals the journey and testimony of the inward struggle of the mind, and the refusal to believe anything that she heard by the doctors and the media, sharing all that she went through on this six month journey with cancer.

Into the Promise is a 30 day devotional for anyone who has been faced with any type of diagnosis, or is standing in faith for any of God's Promises in His Word, bringing Scripture and understanding on how to stand and receive your answer.

Bio

Pastor Pamela Harding is a Minister of God's Word to all who know her. Serving God for over 30 years, she's been a Bible Study teacher for 20 years, an intercessor of prayer in her local schools for 18 years, and now ministers and teaches Healing Classes at Rockford Faith Center, International. Not only was this author completely healed of the cancer, but has also, because of her knowledge of God's Word, been healed of several other diseases, such as rheumatoid arthritis, sjogrens, and fibromyalgia. She's married to her devoted husband, John, for 40 years and they have one son, Paul.

1

Beginning

I'VE BEEN JOURNALING since I was about 16 years old. At that time, I was a messed up, confused teenager that had no set future, no goals, no ambition. Smoking pot didn't help these matters any. I began that when I was 13. Destiny awaits you, but in my case, and at that age, I felt that my destiny was hell, so why bother? God had other plans for me, and thankfully so…*but God.*

I know what it is to believe and not see it yet. *I know* what it is to wait upon the Lord in order for my strength to be renewed. *I know* what it is to battle in the mind with a spirit of death continually lingering over me. *I know* what it is to have to wait, and wait, and wait and still believe that The Word of God is Truth over all my circumstances. And thankfully, ***I know my Redeemer personally***…but God!

2

Background *The Was*

I WAS THE first one born in Illinois; my family had moved here from Missouri. I didn't grow up in church, but my parents had a Christian background and upbringing. Morals and Godly values were high on the list of boundaries that were put into place for us kids. Even though they didn't attend any church, anytime that there were Vacation Bible Schools, or our friends would invite us to church, we were always allowed to go. When my oldest sister married, they began to attend a church in Rockford. I began to go with them and at the age of 9, I became born again, and received the baptism of the Holy Ghost when I was 11. I went to church every chance I got with my sister and brother in law. When I was 13, they moved down south; I was unable to attend any longer.

I tried to live the life of a Christian without anyone in our home living a Godly life. Don't get me wrong, Mom and Dad were good parents, but as far as living in a Christ centered home, that wasn't us. I would go to school and try to share Christ with others, but was ridiculed and made fun of. This wasn't anything strange to me, because I had been over-weight since I was 7. Being called names and teased and bullied added to my being a "Holy Roller." By boldness I found a few others that were also born again. We would periodically get to go to church with them, but that too, would soon end for one reason or another. My life of Christianity ended up with me backsliding. And backslide I did....

Because the church I had attended with my sister was a 'hell fire and damnation' type of preaching, that's what I remembered. More than hearing about Jesus and being able to be forgiven for my sins, I heard damnation. If I sinned at all, I was going straight to hell. So why bother? Not long after, I began to smoke cigarettes and pot was soon to follow. I figured that if I wasn't going to Heaven, then I might as well live like hell. But all the while, I had a nagging feeling like God was always right there watching me; condemnation only moved me further away from Him. The downward slide into drugs and alcohol amped up in my later teens. I kept it hidden very well. I kept my grades up, got an outside job at 16, and stayed within the boundaries that I needed to at home, for the most part.

I met my husband, John, in my junior year. He was a senior. Though he never asked me out at school, I could tell that he was interested, and, I made sure that he knew that I was as well. We ended up marrying the December after I graduated, and the drug party began. We soon began dealing drugs so as to keep up with the addictions. We never made any profit because all of the profit was either smoked or went up our nose. We kept it low key and kept away from family members as much as possible. We successfully avoided answering any questions about our lives. By this time, our family knew what we were doing. Thankfully, we had family that was praying for us; I truly believe that it was those prayers that kept my husband and I alive and out of prison. I said time and time again within myself, that I wouldn't live to see the age of 30 because of all the drugs I was doing. I had no future plans, except to get high.

Cocaine soon became our god. The addiction completely took over. It ruled over us, controlled us, our money, dictated our lives, every waking moment was all about coke, and the next high. I remember praying to God when we would be up pulling all-nighters partying, begging God, "Please don't let me die.", while snorting another line. I have no idea how many times I prayed this, because there were times that I felt my heart beating so fast and hard that I thought it would explode in my chest; it never stopped me from doing another line. When we didn't have the coke, we'd smoke pot, drop acid, pop some speeders, downers, anything for the 'high god' that we were serving. This had become our lives...but God.

3

The Miraculous Deliverance

ONE MORNING, AFTER partying all night, I awoke and something had changed. At the time, I couldn't explain it, but the cocaine addiction was completely gone from me! That afternoon we went to the place that we always partied; the desire to snort another line was over. They cut it up, lined it out, handed me the mirror, and I just let it pass by me. It was finished! Four months later, my husband was miraculously delivered from cocaine too. He never had any kind of background with God, except through me, and that had been very limited. Even though we still smoked pot (and I, cigarettes) and drank occasionally, I began to see things in a different light. I realized that God had delivered me from the cocaine. The only thing I prayed was to not die, yet, He went beyond and delivered John and I both from it.

Knowing and realizing that God had done this for us, I began to search out a church. I was by myself, it didn't make any difference to me. I knew that I had to get God back into my life. I began attending an Assembly of God Church which was very large. I would sit in the very back row. I wanted this to be on my own terms, not because someone was making me. The messages that I was hearing wasn't like the ones I remembered as a child. They spoke of Jesus, our Forgiveness, our Healer, our Deliverer and it caused a greater hunger within me to know Him more.

On my way to Church one Sunday morning, I noticed a new church that had been built not far from our home. It was little and quaint looking; I had quite a sizable offering that Sunday and thought that they could probably use this offering. I decided to go there that Sunday morning. Little did I know, that it would begin a journey that still, to this day, hasn't ended.

4

The teaching of faith

AS I BEGAN to attend New Life Assembly of God, my quaint little church, the couple lead us graduated from Rhema Bible College. They had a rack of Kenneth Hagin books available in the back of the Church for purchase. As I continued to grow and learn about Jesus, I bought every book that was on that rack. God was 'growing me up' in Him. I didn't understand it then, but I was devouring everything I could about faith. In this time in my life, I found out that I had been forgiven. There was no need to run to the Altar to be 'born again, again; I didn't know that my sins had been put as far away as the East is from the West. With a joy that surpassed my own understanding, I sat and soaked in everything that I could.

In 1994 on my way home from Church, I had to stop and get some cigarettes at a gas station. While waiting to turn left, my car was rear ended by a young man going approximately 40 m.p.h. He saw me at the last second, swerved and hit me in the rear of my car. I saw it coming, so I put my brake on hard, I was going to be pushed head on into oncoming traffic of a very busy four lane road. The impact sent my car lunging forward into that traffic but thankfully, the car coming at me head on stopped just in time!

This accident cost me a very good job. For the next five years, doctors were unable to do much to help alleviate the pain from the injuries that I sustained. My A/C joint was impacted and I had dislocated several discs in the top of my spine and the base of my neck. At that time, doctors were uneasy about doing surgery. Thus began the course of pain meds, acupuncture, cortisone shots, spinal blocks, and chiropractors. Nothing worked, especially me. I had always worked; since I was 11 I had a job. John and I depended on two incomes, and my factory jobs allowed me to make a very decent income. Things began to get tense all the way around.

God miraculously supplied all of our needs during this time. My husband wasn't saved yet and the only tithe that I had to give was out of the grocery money. Because I knew that the tenth belonged to God, I tithed each week and offered any extra change that I had in my purse.

John and I had always been responsible to pay our bills, even when we were partying; it was what we had been taught by our parents. We knew that if we wanted a place to live, we'd better stay on top of them. One day a notice arrived; we were being turned over to a collection agency due to the long overdue medical bills that were still accumulating. My insurance company was going after the young man's insurance company to pay all the expenses, but, because of the process of time, John and I were paying anything we could on all of the bills. I stayed in touch with all of them, kept them posted on my insurance company's progress on what was happening with the insurance, and assured them we were paying as much as we could afford; they had records of our calls.

When I received this notice I immediately called the hospital. The woman I spoke with looked up my account and saw that we had been paying monthly. Sometimes it was only $5.00, but she saw that we were trying. She suggested that we fill out a sheet itemizing the income verses the outcome so they could reconsider being turned over to the collections. John, being diligent to stay on top of matters, filled out this sheet. He called me into the room to look at the paperwork. Our outcome exceeded our income, yet we weren't late on any of our bills! He kept refiguring, erasing, filling in, and finally gave up trying to make sense of it. We had the paystubs, bills and records to prove what was on the paperwork. I just praised God for His Provision and left the room, knowing exactly what I and John just witnessed....but God! The favor of God didn't stop there. The hospital received our paperwork and said that they would wait for the insurance payoff as long as we would continue to pay what we could monthly! We never received another notice concerning these matters again, even though it took seven years to receive a settlement for the accident.

During this time, I tried to get jobs after being off work for almost a year. Everything would go well in the interviews until they found out that I had a doctors restriction because of the injuries. Finally, a fast food chain took a chance and hired me for drive through register.

I continued to go to Church, believing God would heal me, after all, it's what His Word said; I was a believer, so I trusted that it would happen. Somewhere after three years of taking pain meds, I heard the Lord tell me to start saving my medicine bottles when they were emptied. Wasn't sure why, but I obeyed.

I was desperate, at my end and had no other place to turn but to God for my healing. The doctors had let me know that there was nothing else they could do. I was told about two very dynamic women who were teaching a healing class at a local church. I began around the middle of October, attended every Saturday morning, with these classes going until May. They taught on Covenant, how it was my inherited right to healing and deliverance, that Satan was trying to destroy, and this was a fight of faith. They suited all of us in class up with the Armor of God and His Weapons. Prayer Scriptures and declarations were lined up on the tables for us to take home and use during the week. There were many that had cancer. One young man in particular, was only 32 years old, was married with 2 young girls; he had been diagnosed with 4th stage prostate cancer and told that he only had about 2 weeks left to live. He had come to that church where these two teachers ministered at the Altar. Thankfully, he came forward, gave his life to Christ, and learned about the healing classes.

I was amazed as I watched all of us continue to encourage each other and grow, and this young man, every week, was there. His death sentence of two weeks came and went, all the while, he was taking chemo and radiation, not one hair fell off of his head! God was doing an amazing work in each of us, and my healing came by the end of that session. The young man? He wasn't at the last class because he had taken his family to Disneyland. He had been completely healed from the cancer! My testimony was given at the end, I realized why I had been told to keep the empty bottles, for these were a testimony of how Faithful God was to me. They filled up a large wicker basket; I still have them and use them when I teach...but God.

Because of how God was moving in my life, my Pastors saw the Anointing that I had and asked me to teach one night. Teaching became a regular for me on Wednesday nights. I kept pressing in and forward with what God was teaching me. I began to 'see' things in the Spirit. I could see what God's Desire was for His Body and the urgency I had to get His Message out to whomever would listen.

5

A Bible study begins

IN 1998, I began working in a public school cafeteria. During this time, I shared my faith in Jesus Christ with whomever would listen. Fortunately I had a captive audience because of the size of our kitchen. About a year into the job, I heard the Spirit tell me one morning to start a Bible Study in my home. I replied, "You bring the people to attend it then." I left it at that. About two weeks later, a woman at work approached me. She said that she had met a woman who was asking her a lot of questions about God, and that she wasn't sure how to answer her. She had told her about me and decided to ask if I would be interested in starting a Bible Study with both of them. God is Amazing! Where He gives the vision, He also gives the Provision! So, I did. Here I am 20 years later, still having a home Bible Study. The one who asked for me to have the study, is still attending.

I have seen well over 200 to 300 people, maybe more, come and go in our home through the years. Grateful to have another opportunity to share the Gospel with people, I sensed that our home was a training camp. I wasn't tickling peoples' ears when I taught or preached. I have always taught the uncompromised Word of God, and because of this, many would begin to attend, but as soon as they felt that it was "too radical", or they didn't like it because I would challenge their false beliefs and systems, they wouldn't return. One thing that I had said to the Lord was that I wasn't going to chase anyone down to get them to come. Whoever was supposed to be here would be here. I truly believed that my steps were and still are ordered by the Lord, so I've always trusted that He would bring whomever needed to hear what I was saying. Week after week, throughout all these years, I've never had a meeting where nobody showed up. I've had one class with only one person, once, but even then, I truly believed that God had predestined for us to be alone because of the way the Holy Spirit ministered to them through me.

During this time, I had learned how to flow in the Anointing. Prophetic teachings began to be released through me and I began to see things that were to come in the future. I'm not someone special, but because of what the Word of God says we should ask Him of things to come concerning His Sons and Daughters, and ask Him for His Super on our natural. My foundation was built week after week, stronger and stronger. My faith was greatly developed during these years of many tribulations and circumstances. He brought my family and I through all of them, proving Himself faithful to His Word. He never let us down. All the while, John wasn't part of the classes, nor did he go to Church with me, even though I would try to preach to him.

One Sunday morning, after telling John that he needed to get up and go to Church, I heard the Holy Spirit forcefully and sternly say, "SHUT UP!!! YOU ARE DRIVING HIM AWAY FROM ME, NOT TO ME!" Boy, did I hear that! From then on, I would restrain my tongue from saying anything about God to John. I had to let go of the responsibility for bringing John in. That was a great lesson learned because that is exactly what God began to do, bring John in.

6

John's Salvation

WHEN THE MOVIE, *The Passion of Christ* came out, our Church rented the whole theatre in our city, allowing us to buy tickets from them. There was a lot of talk in the media about this movie and the stir that it was making. My husband was curious, and I recognized this, so I asked if he wanted to see it with me. He accepted. He knew that I had gotten the tickets through Church, but, surprisingly, he went anyway.

John hadn't grown up in Church, had no religious background, other than going once with a neighbor to his Church. This was, according to John, one of *those* Holy Roller Churches, and it scared the Dickens out of him! He never wanted anything to do with Church because of this. The only Word of God that he got was when he overheard me teach the Bible Study, or heard when I listened to Christian teaching tapes. I was really surprised, but thankful, that he wanted to see this movie with me. God had been moving in John's life unbeknownst to me after He had told me to shut up. When our Pastor gave an Altar call at the end of the movie, John accepted Christ into his heart that night! God still didn't allow me much in the way of teaching him, because I had learned a great lesson through my husband. God didn't need my help this time. But God.

7

Settling in With Disease

If you settle for what you've got, you deserve what you have....

SOMETIME AROUND 2013, I was having difficulty with various symptoms in my body. Things were getting worse. I could tell that more and more, some things were wrong and I needed to see a doctor. So I made an appointment, had some blood work done by a neurologist, and was diagnosed with 7 different diseases, most of them genetic. I did not resist these diagnoses, I just accepted what he said and left with the prescriptions. I had decided that being the woman of faith that I was, I would just accept the reports, take the medications prescribed and just let it all be. No battling with the Word, after all, the Word said I was already healed; I just settled in with what was. Looking back, I was about to learn a very valuable lesson from all of this, but not until the next diagnosis came.

8

Diagnosis: 3rd stage lung cancer into the lymph nodes......But God!

If we knew of the journey, would we stay on the path?

IF SOMEONE WOULD'VE asked me that question 20 years ago, knowing what I do today, I wonder if I would. Ask me that now, on this side of those 20 years, over and over the answer would be an astounding; " YES!!!"

In March of 2015, I became ill and was told that I had pneumonia. After several rounds of antibiotics, it still lingered, which caused my physician to order a CT scan. I had faith in God that all would be well and tried not to think much of it, after all, I knew that by the Stripes of Jesus Christ, as a Covenant believer, that I was already healed. So when it came back that there was a mass in the right upper lobe of my lung, I knew the battle was on. I stood on the Promise of God, declaring that it was going to be benign, when they said that the mass would need to be biopsied.

As a Bible teacher for almost 17 years in my home, at that time, I had a very good foundation built upon the Word of God. My teaching was recognized by the leadership of my Church, and I was blessed to be able to teach the 'Build Your Foundation' class with my brother in Christ, Jeff. We were a tag team, you might say, because there were eight topics that we taught, one of those being 'The Covenant', which I was blessed to teach. Little did I know then how much I was going to have to rely upon that foundation that I thought I was teaching others. I taught on how to build a Covenant relationship with God, but all the while, it was being built in me.

My husband John and I knew that the call was going to be coming about the CT scan on the following Wednesday; we stayed close to the phone. We believed God to come through for us on this. The phone rang later that afternoon and it was the doctor's office. The nurse was calling, and I quickly said to her, "Well, I believe that I'm receiving the report of the Lord." She agreed with me and then began to read the report out loud to me. After hearing herself say, "Stage 3 non-small cell lung cancer.." after she had just agreed with me, she realized what she had just read. She quickly began to stammer and you could hear the fear in her voice. "I am so sorry Pam, I had no idea that this would be...." It was funny because I immediately began to console her, and told her that I am going to be just fine; I was already healed and God would see to this, even though I was reeling inside.

After hanging up, I was numb and dumbfounded. John was sitting right across the room from me and could tell by my reaction that it wasn't good. All I told him was that it was non-small cell lung cancer. For the first time in a long time, I was at a loss for words. John came over, pulled me close and told me that everything was going to be alright, that we were in this thing together.

9

Sleeping with the Giants

NOT LONG AFTER the diagnosis of cancer, the Holy Spirit began to deal with me about all the other diseases that were still there, in which I had done nothing. Numbers 33:55 suddenly was brought to my attention; *"But if you will not drive out the inhabitants of the land from before you; then it shall come to pass, that those which ye let remain of them shall be pricks, in your eyes and thorns in your sides, and shall vex you in the land which you dwell."* Suddenly my eyes were opened to Truth. My belief that it was all just going to go away, with no work on my part was a deception. This wasn't faith with works, this was literally laying down with those giants that were trying to steal, kill and destroy my life.

I had the Revelation of my flesh being the Promised Land several years before during a teaching. The 'earthen vessels' spoken about in 2 Corinthians 4:7 are us. God formed us out of dirt. Every Promise of Covenant given to us, are to come to this land we live in, physically and Spiritually. The Revelation plus the Word of God being Seed that we plant in our hearts, is how we will receive the Promises that God said was ours. Our Covenant agreement of accepting Jesus Christ as our Lord and Savior, agreeing with His Word, speaking His Word alone and being renewed in our minds, we become the proof and evidence of God's Good and Perfect Will for mankind on Earth to be revealed. (Romans 12:2). Knowing all of this, yet doing nothing, was allowing the giants of disease to occupy my land. This is where the battle truly began.

10

The Journey of Healing

I WORKED IN a public school system, allowing us off for the summer, thankfully. I had time to seek the Lord in this matter. He began to reveal Scriptures to me about how I was able to take in any deadly thing and it would not harm me, how I was already healed by the Stripes of Jesus Christ and that I had nothing to fear. I had heard it said, "We can't stop the birds from flying overhead, but we can stop them from nesting in our hair." Believe me, the negative thoughts and doubts were flying! I had already determined that I was going to dig in my heels and not let those thoughts prevail, I was to do as it says in Proverbs 4:-20-27. I was to keep my eyes focused on Jesus and not let the Word of God depart from before my eyes, to keep them in the midst of my heart because it was life for me and health to my flesh. It also says to "put away a forward mouth and perverse lips." I praise God for I had already been doing this for several years, and guarded my thoughts and my words, and did not allow anything that was contrary to the Word of God to come out of my mouth. God gave me the strategy; I was going at this day by day.

One of the most important things that He spoke to me was to not let my hand go before His steps that were ordered for me. I had to stay in this place with Him moment by moment, trusting Him sometimes, moment by moment, and that He was going to get me through this completely; it was only for a season. Before meeting with any doctors,

I knew that I was to take the chemo and radiation treatments, but was not going to have any surgery. That which Satan had met for my harm, God had told me He was going to baffle the medical community with all of this, for His Glory. Sometimes I just wish God would let us know just how He plans on doing these things before He does them. This was the moment by moment that He had spoken of.

I was very careful as to who I was going to release this information to. Because my husband was a newer Christian, he didn't even know that it was 3rd stage lung cancer and in the lymph nodes. Because of understanding spiritual battles, it mattered with whom I linked spiritual armor with, meaning who and what I said to people. If I would've linked with people who were more world minded instead of Word of God minded, their lack of knowledge sway them to be sympathizers; this would've pulled me back instead of advancing with me into the manifestation of my victory in this flesh over this disease. I had to fortify my Shield of Faith with strong brothers and sisters in Christ who believed the same way that I did. I only told a few people in my family and my Apostles and Leadership about the diagnosis. I told them I did not want them asking me how I was doing, because if I was already healed and whole, that question was unnecessary. No matter what it looked like, they would not move from their Covenant stance of faith in the Blood of Jesus for me. I asked my Apostle, who is Head Leader of my Church and my Spiritual Father, 10 days after the diagnosis, if I could have the platform when this was all said and done to give my testimony of how God had healed me. His reply was, "Absolutely."

Appointments were made for me with a surgeon, a radiologist, and an oncologist. Knowing what I do about Covenant, I know that even shaking my head yes means agreement, so before seeing any of them, I had determined that I would not do this; I declared to each one of them that I was already healed by the Stripes of Jesus Christ. I told them I understood what they were saying to me, but I did not agree with them. As I listened to each one of them, the surgeon and oncologist received what I said, the radiologist, not so much. The three had already met with one another concerning my case and had decided that I should take chemo and radiation treatments first, and then have surgery. I already knew what path I was going to take.

Because of the Scripture in Mark 16:18 that says we are able to take in any deadly thing and it will not harm us, I knew in my Spirit that I was to lay hands and pray over every x-ray machine, every medication, every treatment and declare it to be blessed to the good only of my body and that it would not harm me in any way, and then praise God and thank Him that I was already healed. I was to do this out loud and in front of every person around. So, I was ready to go, beginning with the radiation and chemo.

I was nervous as I drove to my first set of treatments, but during all of this, I had such a peace within me. The hospital was remodeling the building where I was going to spend a lot of time at for the next several months. At the very top of the entryway the sign said, "Center for Cancer Care. Temporary Entrance." Praise God, talk about a true sign from God; this was only temporary! I checked in and they led me back to an area where I was to change into a gown. In this area were little cubicles and under each cubicle, were the first name and initial of the last name of those who were receiving treatment. As I changed into the gown, I began laying hands and praying over each one of these cubicles and declaring healing for every one of them. I committed to pray daily over each one of these ladies.

Soon, one of the technicians came in and called my name to take me back for my first radiation treatment. I told her as we went back that I was a Christian and was believing that I was already healed, letting her know that before anything happened that I was going to lay hands on that machine to pray over it, which I did. There was another technician in the room with her, and they both bowed their heads as I prayed. When I laid down on that machine after praying over it, I had a flash vision happen to me. I saw Jesus Christ come in and lay down on top of me, facing the same direction I was facing. I was completely hidden inside of Him, when He turned His Head to the right and said to me, "I've already done this for you." Great peace and warmth came over me. After the radiation, I was taken upstairs to start the chemo. Again, I let the nurses know that were going to oversee my treatments, what I would be doing daily, and they were not to give me anything without my praying over it and laying hands on it first to bless it. Thankfully, not one of these technicians or nurses got in the way, but bowed their heads as I prayed.

God continued to confirm His Promises to me with numerous signs and wonders happening throughout this journey. He was bringing people across my pathway that I was able to encourage and pray for while we were in the waiting areas for the treatments. On the 3rd day of the treatments, I noted as I prayed over the cubicles, a new name had been put on one of the cubicles. Thelma S. What was amazing about this was that my Mother's name, Thelma S(houlders)! Once again the peace of God and the warmth in my heart of my Mother's love overwhelmed me. I actually got to meet Thelma S. in the waiting room several days later, and was able to pray with her personally, which truly was a blessing for me.

Another wonder that happened during this time pertained to birds. My husband and I watch over the birds, and take care of them, so we pay a lot of attention to them. We have hummingbird feeders that hang all around our deck and they bring us a lot of joy. One night, right after the diagnosis, I was returning home from Sunday night service at church. Dusk was just starting to settle in when my husband called me and told me there was a humming bird hanging upside down on one of our feeders. He was able to approach it and it wouldn't move. I was just a few miles from home when he called, and the bird was still there when I arrived. I handed John my phone as we walked up very close to the bird to take a picture. He snapped a few close-up shots when all of a sudden, another hummingbird darted at my face! I couldn't believe that this bird, who normally is a rival at our feeders was protecting this other bird! We decided to leave them alone and come in for the night. The next morning when I went out to leave to go to another chemo & radiation treatment, the bird was still there! I heard the Holy Spirit say, "Just as I have kept this bird safe in the darkness, so am I keeping you." When I returned, he was gone.

I also had robins landing all around me. Now, in this region where I live, they are only here for a couple of seasons in the spring and summer, and leave as the days start turning colder. Seeing robins all around me wasn't what amazed me, but what they were doing around me was. First, there were three trying to make nests right up next to our home, under our deck. We would no sooner take down their nests, only for them to come right back and find them building again! Or, I would go out to mow the grass and one would land right in front of my mower while it was running! I would be sitting on my deck, and one would land on the rail right next to me. Trust me, this is not normal! It was happening quite regularly, unlike I had ever experienced before. Remembering what God had said, it was only for a season, just as these birds represented to us, a season.

Soon, the days turned into weeks, and the weeks began to turn into months. I began to lose my hair. I had no idea how much hair I had until it began to fall out! The Scripture says that God knows the numbers of hairs that I had, as it states in Matthew 10:30. I had a very thick head of hair and had loosely filled 4 small garbage cans with it, between the washing and brushing it. I was looking in the mirror at myself, most of my hair now gone, with only patches here and there left. While standing there, I heard the Holy Spirit say to me that He knew when the 47th strand fell out. He knew when the 468th fell out, that this was how familiar He was with me. I was absolutely amazed as I went to the Word in Matthew 10:30 & Luke 12:7 and found it that it was true! I had always just read that He knew how many strands I had, not that He had numbered each one of them! To think that He was this mindful of me, only made me stand more in awe of Him. All along, I never stopped praising God and thanking Him for each day He had blessed me with, and for all of His Mercies that sufficiently supplied every need I would have for that day. I refused to complain about anything!

The time had come when I had to take a leave of absence from work. I only told the people that needed to know what was going on, that I was declaring my healing, and I would be back soon. They were no strangers to my faith and my belief in Christ, having ministered to most of them in the past. I let them who had to know what was going on that they were not to tell anyone about it. Mari Jo, head of Human Resources, who also is a Christian, asked me when I thought then that I would return. I told her off the top of my head, not having a calendar in front of me, November 6th. She wrote it down and said she was standing with me for my healing.

Miraculously, the effects of these treatments, other than losing my hair, weren't happening to me like they were in those who were going through the same journey. I was still able to clean my home, take care my yard, and function normally with very little weakness happening! I didn't lose my appetite or have the nausea and sickness happen from the chemo, amazingly. I was still laying hands on everything, every day, and making daily confessions and declarations saying that no harm would come to me, that God was my Strength, my Healer, my Deliverer, my Peace and my Joy! I dove into the Word, knowing that this was the way I was going to receive the blessing of God's Promises for me and my life. I had people telling me that I looked better than I had looked in a long time! I was weekly seeing the oncologist, who was a Muslim, but yet very encouraging to me. He would see me and say, "You look amazing!" To which I would reply, "God is so good," and he would respond, "God is great!" Now I knew that his god and my God were not the same, but he didn't argue, so I left it alone. The radiologist, who also was a Muslim, was becoming more and more frustrated with me and I could tell it. I don't think he liked my saying that I was doing well. Which I really was! I continued to state that I was already healed by the Stripes of Jesus Christ, and that I wouldn't receive any other report but the Lord's.

One morning he came in and began to tell me what I should be expecting to happen. I sat and listened, with my chin resting on my fist, refusing to nod my head as he went on. When he finished I looked at him and said, "I understand what you're saying, but I don't agree. I am already healed and I am trusting my God." He stood up to leave the office, extending his hand to shake mine and very irritated, said again what I was to expect. I grabbed his hand to shake it, turned it over and patted the back of it and said, "Bless your heart, I'm already healed." He just walked out.

The Word of God says for me to keep It ever before my eyes, so, that's what I did. I was writing Scriptures on postcards and hanging them up all over my house, my bathroom, in my refrigerator, in my office, on my dresser in my bedroom. The Word of God was ever before my eyes! For years I have declared Scriptures over mine and my family's lives, knowing that the Word of God has the power in Itself to bring Itself to pass. Since I was writing Scriptures down that were speaking to me whenever I would do my prayer time, I had notes everywhere. One Monday morning I decided to organize them in a Microsoft Word document on my computer. If you are familiar with this program you know that you can choose a font and a size before you begin a document. I had chosen to use the font 'Calibri (Body) at a size 14. I wasn't able to complete it that day, so I just minimized it for the time being.

Tuesday night I was awakened with symptoms manifesting in my body, and when anything like this happened, I began to immediately declare the Word of God and telling the symptoms to stop and for my body to line up with what the Bible says. But for some reason this night, I said something different. I knew that what I had said had come from the Holy Spirit. I quickly went into the office to type it out. As I sat down, I brought the document up on my computer that I had been writing the Scriptures on, began typing and realized that the font and size had changed. I looked and now instead of 'Calibri (Body) 14', it had changed to 'inherit 12'! I was stunned! When I saw that, I knew it was a miracle from God, for several reasons. One of them being, that I just "happened" to be teaching at that time to my Bible group about inheriting the Covenant Promises of God. I also know that numbers in the Bible represent different Biblical Truths, and the number 12 represents Godly Governmental Authority! I went back to bed, but it took quite a while to go back to sleep, because of what had just happened.

The following Monday, I went back to this document to finish it up. Because of this miracle font that just happened to appear, I decided to highlight the whole document to change all of it into that 'inherit 12' font. When I did, suddenly, a drop-down window popped up saying that there was no such font! I tried it again, but again, it wouldn't let me. With technology being what it is today, I went on the internet to search for the 'inherit' font. *There isn't one.* Anywhere! None of the software available for making word documents has an inherit font! Over and over God was letting me know that He was right here with me through it all.

The week of November 2nd came, and it was time to have another CT scan. I had an appointment scheduled with the radiologist for Friday, November 5th for the results. To be honest, I was nervous about the appointment, but still had perfect peace within my spirit. On Wednesday, November 3rd, I received a phone call early that morning. It was a Pastor and mentor from my Church, who also is a firm believer in the Word of God, and one of the few that knew the diagnosis. When I answered all he said was, "Hallelujah! Hallelujah! Hallelujah! repeating this 7 times, then blessed me and hung up! No, I didn't think this strange of him, because I know that this is a man of God who hears clearly and is directed by the Holy Spirit, so I knew this was from God through him.

My husband, up until this time, had not been going with me to any of my appointments. I wouldn't let him, because if everything was going well in our lives, he would normally be at work. This was what he was supposed to do, if we really believed that I was already healed. This time, John wanted to go with me, I agreed knowing he'd be meeting the radiologist for the first time. I had warned John about this doctor's attitude toward me, but wasn't expecting what this doctor said to my husband upon meeting him. When he walked into the room,

I introduced my husband to him. He extended his hand to shake his and said, "I'm not sure if you're her better half or not." I just looked at John with a wink and an 'I told you so,' nod. The doctor then proceeded to sit down at his computer, asking how things were going for me. I repeated that all was well, as I had in the past. I wanted to know what the results were, and he seemed to be delaying for some reason. Finally, I just asked what the results were from the CAT scan. He then turned the computer screen to me, showing the scan results and said, "A picture is worth a 1000 words." There were my scans with no more highlights in them. The cancer was gone, completely gone! I raised my hands up to Heaven, and began to weep and praise God for His Promise that He had fulfilled for me. I then grabbed John and hugged him, who also was crying and praising God with me. I turned around and looked at the doctor, who came over to me and hugged me, never saying another word about it. That was okay, he didn't have to. God had the last word.

(By the way, one more miracle occurred this day that I realized later. Did you notice the date I received the report of the Lord? If you remember, I told the woman in Human Resources that I would return to work on November 6th. Chalk another one up for God!)

11

Giving up the fight
for the Victory battle

I **KNEW** I had been battling with a spirit of death for a long time, especially after the diagnosis of cancer. At times it would lessen, yet in the back of my mind it was always there. Strange to live life wondering if you're going to really be having a life to live. I mean, I had resolved in my Spirit man that I would live long on Earth, holding fast to God's Promises, yet all the while living in a body that was fighting me all the way...dread, dread, it was heavy. One of the previous diagnoses was restrictive lung disease. My Mother had died from this and my Dad had heart disease and emphysema. Mental torment was something that I had to resist. I would have to stop the thoughts that came over and over telling me that I was going to die just like my Mother did. Guarding my heart from the voices in my head became a daily task. Especially now, since the radiation in the lung area had further affected my breathing. Any physical movement would result in shortness of breath and it was a fight to do anything. I didn't have the freedom to just get up, walk across the room, get a book, and go back to read it without my mind thinking about all the exertion to do only that. But I would press through it, resisting the dread and do it anyway. The strength of ability for that day by day living was becoming physically less and less.

Right before the following experience, I remember saying to God that I needed His help to keep fighting this. I was growing weary and just felt like I didn't have much left in me to keep on keeping on. I said to Him; "Father, I have to let go and just believe that You will give me tomorrow. That it's not my adamantly holding on with everything I have to get it, but that just because You said it, I'll have it. Regardless, I'm letting go and letting You."

Saturday evening came and I attended a business meeting at Church. When I came in, John was watching television, so I went to the kitchen to grab a bite to eat. Soon after, he told me that his show was over, come into the living room with him and relax and watch something that I wanted. Several weeks before, one of my sister's had sent a link to a website of Classic T.V. programs from the 50's. I'm always looking for anything simple, relaxing and clean to watch, and I hadn't had a chance to check this website out yet. I connected the computer to the television, started to sort through the programs. They were all black and white shows from the early 50's, mostly game shows and a few situation comedies. My husband and I would start one, watch about 10 minutes or so, then go onto another. These were before our time, so we were amused by what we saw. While watching one of them, the thought went through my mind, "I wonder how many of these people are dead?" I immediately cast that thought out and went on watching these grainy, poorly put together programs. After about 40 minutes of several, we gave it up and went up to bed.

John and I had been sick for a couple of days with a respitory flu, so coughing was a factor whenever we'd lay down. Well, this night, surprisingly, John went right to sleep, and I plugged in my healing Scriptures set to music, listening through my earbuds. Usually, I fall asleep pretty quickly, but this night, that deep sleep was eluding me for some reason. My Spirit was very attentive to the Scriptures that I was listening to. I was just going into that sleep where your mind just kind of runs within itself, when I saw all these faces in a semi-circle of the people I had just been watching in these old black and whites. They were in a dark background, they themselves were in black and white and they were smiling and laughing at me, as if welcoming me there. I remember thinking, 'Oh, do you want me to join you?" Then it began.

Suddenly, I was surrounded by all these black and white beings that were on the television, men, women, young and old, all of their faces very grainy, demonic, and their features kept contorting before me. All of them were taunting, tormenting poking at me, yet never touching me. They would come within inches of my being, their faces up in mine, going round and round about me. Somewhere in this time, I said, "Are any of you believers in Christ Jesus?" None seemed to reply as they relentlessly continued. I began to cough, rising up out of bed. I sat up instantly knowing something was off. Something was wrong. I looked around my room but it was as if it was distant from me. I immediately got out of bed and said very firmly, "John!" No reply! This was not like my husband at all, as he has been very attentive to me and my needs because of the health status that I had been in. I walked around to him and touched him, speaking more firmly, "JOHN!" Quickly he awoke, sat up and asked, "What's wrong?" "I don't know, something is wrong. I don't know what it is. This is not right." "What's not right?", he asked as he reached out to take my vitals. I wasn't panicking, breathing hard, my heart was beating normally, no sweats, and as a matter of fact, I felt nothing in my body! I couldn't feel my body! I sensed that everything was working properly, yet having no attachment of feeling going on in my body. He asked if I wanted to go downstairs, which we did.

We sat down together on the loveseat. He put his arm around me, as I began to look around the room. The room was there, everything was the same, but I wasn't present in it. No feeling from within, and I just kept saying, something is wrong, something is wrong. I tried to evaluate my situation within; should I go to the emergency room? And if I did, what would I tell them? I couldn't even explain what was going on to my husband or myself, much less a doctor! So that was out. John went to get me a glass of water. I took a drink and as John was walking away from me, I said, "I have to say this, and out loud. I bind the spirit of death off of me right now in Jesus Name!" John sat down next to me, put his hand on the back of my neck and said, "Pam, you have the Spirit of Life!" I remember turning my head and looking out at him, thinking, did he just say what he did? When suddenly I realized that I was separate from my body and I was actually inside of it looking out!

I sat there for a moment, taking in what I had just realized was going on. I wasn't afraid, everything was surreal. Being in my living room, but seeing it through a different dimension, I was in it, yet I wasn't...

I told John to go to bed and I proceeded to move across the room to the recliner. He replied that he was going to stay with me on the couch until I was ready to go up. He shut the lights off, but I was still able to see my surroundings. Nothing changed, so I thought I'd just go back up to where all this started in the first place, back to bed. Laying down on my side, John's hand was continually touching me on my back, due to his concern. As I lay there, I realized that I was being elevated. Pockets of air masses, like pillows, were raising me up and I knew that there was a current of air beneath me that was lifting me through the darkness. It felt like when I was riding a roller coaster and going up that first major hill towards the top before dropping. I remember my stomach sensing the movement and doing a bit of a flip within. Suddenly I stopped. My new surroundings were smoky and mystical like and still dark. It was then that I felt 'hands' plunge into my chest which began to massage my lungs. It was such warmth and healing being massaged into them. My lungs, for the first time in several years, felt good, all the pressure, the ache within them was gone. I was just enjoying the euphoria of that moment when I realized that there was this beautiful Angel standing before me. It was as if a light went on in a theatre. She was bronze and dressed regally, with a brass type headdress and bronze armor on, Cleopatra like. She held a long, thin trumpet of gold in her hands that had two flags suspended from the end, one white, one red. I looked to her left right in front of me and I saw the most beautiful landscape; vivid colors of blue, green and bright yellow-white fields before me. It was set away from me in the distance with a city beyond the landscape. At the time, I was enthralled with what I was seeing, but it didn't dawn on me until later, that it was the Kingdom of God before me.

The Angel lifted the trumpet to her lips to blow. As she did, I heard, "From this night onward, your life has been Altered, your healing has now begun. You are changed, daughter of Zion."

I began to cough and sat up in bed, realizing that I was back. The time on my alarm clock read 3:33.

12

The Is: *I AM HEALED*

THE PROBLEM IS that man has not developed their personal relationship with the Great I AM to understand Kingdom Principles. They have not established a relationship of trust and faithfulness that one finds when they spend quality time with their King Jesus through His Word and prayer. A solid foundation is formed when we develop and mature in His Word of Truth. There arises the Truth of the Word within and the Wisdom and Understanding that Holy Spirit gives to us as we continue to pursue our relationship with One another. It is this Oneness that you become, in time, with Him. So when you say, "I AM healed!", this Oneness supersedes any circumstance and lie of the devil that comes our way. The phrase, 'I AM healed,' (His Part) and 'I AM healed,' (my part) becomes your Revelational Truth that cannot separate the Great I AM from oneself! You really do become the Word made flesh, I AM HEALED. It was He that healed you so that you now are healed and can truthfully say, "I AM HEALED!" The very prayer that Jesus prayed in John 17 of our Oneness with Him and with one another becomes who you are!

Jesus had to release this prayer while on Earth as a man. It is one of God's Ways to establish His Word and make it manifest here that He has chosen. Man has to speak it out into the atmosphere by faith in order for it to manifest in the Earth realm. Psalms 103:20: "Bless the Lord, ye His angels, that excel in strength, that do His Commandments, hearkening unto the voice of His Word." I LOVE this Scripture! This is a way of God's Oneness in us through Christ Jesus! He has chosen to give us the Authority and responsibility of speaking His Word out of our mouths. As soon as we speak *His Word,* (note, the angels hearken to His Word) and *remain* without wavering that Word we spoke, His angels, are waiting upon His Word to be spoken, immediately go to bring that Word to pass in our lives. We were given this Revelation in Daniel 10:12. Hebrews 13:8 says that Jesus Christ is the same yesterday, today and forever, so He *never* changes, therefore, His Ways and His Word doesn't change either. Our ability to become 'One with Him' wouldn't and couldn't happen if Jesus hadn't established through prayer; He decreed this Truth of God's Original Plan and intent for mankind out loud while He was still a man. God had given man all dominion for Earth in Genesis 1:26 when He created us in His Image. This was a Spirit-soul-body man when He established it. But unfortunately, man failed and gave his godship and dominion over to Satan when he shared the fruit from the Tree of Knowledge of Good and Evil. Eve was deceived, but the sin (curse) came when Adam ate, becoming a body-soul-spiritually dead man. No more connection to the Life Giver. You see, Adam & Eve had already become one with each other, which is a Spiritual Truth, therefore, both had to fall when they partook of the fruit. When they fell, they fell from a living Spirit-soul-body to body-soul-spiritually dead. So did every man born into this World after them. But Praise be to God that Adam's dominion and godship was re-established when Jesus came to Earth. God's Original Intent of mankind ruling and having dominion over the Earth through His Kingdom Principles was given back to those who had become born again. This immediately put us back to the Spirit-soul-body Truth of who we really are in Christ Jesus. God now sees us and backs us with all of Heaven to see that His Word is ruling over our lives and the lives of those around us by faith.

We are not natural having a Spiritual experience, we are Spiritual having a natural experience. The Spirit realm is everything over this natural realm, everything we need, now being born again (John 3:3, which says that you CANNOT see the Kingdom without being born again) and the Kingdom of God is within us! (Luke 17:21) Now we have access to all of Heavens bountiful storehouses of Provision (Eph. 2:19) in order to have all things that pertain unto life and Godliness as we believe Him and the Word of Truth that He has given to us. (2 Peter 1:3) We have to now grow and learn the ways of God, and, how the Kingdom He rules from works.

13

Disengaging the enemy by the renewal of my mind

YOU SEE, I am rather adamant and strong headed when it comes to the Word of God. When I was a child, I remember singing,.. "If Jesus said it, I believe it, His Word cannot lie. If it's written in the Bible, I'll believe it til I die. Though the mountains be removed and cast into the sea, God's Word will last forever, throughout Eternity." And that has been my stance throughout my walk with Him. Whenever battles in the mind would say otherwise, I would cast those thoughts down and out and replace them with the Promises of God, whatever that might be, as it says in 2 Corinthians 10:5. As I did this and declaring what the Word of God says about me, transformation was taking place, many times without my knowing it. I was becoming the Word, a living Epistle, read of all men. (2 Corinthians 3:2-5) This means that His Word, because I was becoming the physical proof of God's Word, was able to be seen by people who know me. Because what His Promises' were for me, now was happening to me!

Throughout my journey in the Word, God was teaching me how to 'disengage' the enemy of my soul.

The number one factor to all of this was to "...be renewed in the spirit of your mind." Romans 4:23. In Verse 22 it says that we must put off the former conversation. So then what do we put in place of those former conversations? *The Word of God!* The Word of God has the Power of God in It to bring Itself to pass. This must be the first and foremost renewal of our minds, what we speak, what we think; all has to line up with the Word of God. Our words are full of power, some, the very Power of God, because man was created in God's Image. Therefore, we have creative power! "The Power of life and death are in the tongue." (Proverbs 18:21) Deuteronomy 30:19 says that we are to choose life. One has to 'rightly divide' the Word of God, so there are mysteries and hidden treasures that are within the Word, waiting for us to find them. You have to put the Scriptures together, such as a puzzle, so as to see what the Spirit of God is saying to us. Let the Word of God interpret Itself.

Even the world says that you are what you say you are. They didn't come up with this on their own. No, the Word of God says it in Mark 11:23-24. Whatever you pray (say), believe that you receive them and you *shall* have them. Whether good or bad (because we have partaken through Adam, the Tree of Knowledge of Good & Evil), it will come to be in our lives as we think and say. Again, the Word of God says that "...as a man thinks in his heart, so is he." (Proverbs 23:7) Matthew 6:31 says for us…"to take no thought saying…." Most of the time we think before we speak, as it should be! Because I've certainly spoke without thinking first, and trouble came because of that. God is telling us to pay attention to our thoughts. And don't speak whatever comes through our mind, we've got to speak His Word if we want His Blessing and Promises. He's not responsible for what our lives are like; WE ARE! But when we speak only His Word, then He will bring what we're speaking into our lives. For this, He's responsible. I do my part, and trust, KNOWING that He'll do His.

I am responsible for continually renewing my mind. I found out that my mind isn't my brain! My brain is an organ in this earthen vessel. My mind, though, is connected to my soul, which is connected to my heart. In the mind is where wavering takes place. When I have doubt in my mind, it closes my heart of faith to receive the Promises that I'm confessing. I have to renew my mind and this will continue to go on until the day I go to be with Christ.

THE NATURAL MIND CANNOT RECEIVE THE THINGS OF GOD. SO YOU MUST BELIEVE IT IN YOUR HEART THAT YOU ARE HEALED!

There was a woman that my husband and I had known for at least 20 years who called me out of the blue one early morning. I hadn't spoken with her for many years, when she began to share that she was in the 4th stage of cancer and on the death bed. She was a Christian and God had put me on her heart, directing her to call me. She had no idea that God had just healed me of cancer. I began to share my testimony and the Word of God with her. She knew all of this, saying that she hadn't applied the Word of Faith to her situation until she was in the grips of this horrid disease. Encouraged by the call, she hung up with the information that I had shared with her, believing God for her healing.

The following month, my husband and I were getting ready for bed when he told me that she had passed away from cancer. He didn't know that I had spoken with her, as there are some things that I keep just between the Lord and I. I began to grieve inwardly for her, trying to make some sense out of all of this. I had been ministering to several other Christians who had cancer who also passed away. Within myself I said to the Lord, "But by the Grace of God go I." Suddenly, rushing up from within me, with a very loud, stern voice I heard, "**NO! Yes, My Grace supplied it, but you had to take it!**" I laid in bed for quite a while that night hearing that said over and over in my Spirit.

I had been asking God and wanting to know the "how come I lived and not them" question with every person that I was ministering to that had ended up dying. Even though they knew the Word of God, many having been in Church their whole lives, I didn't understand. Good, wonderful women and men who loved God wholeheartedly, yet never received their healing. They believed, yet died. It wasn't enough. And I wanted to know why.

Even now, as I'm writing this, God has been teaching me all along the Principles of His Kingdom and how to access It. And I'm still learning. When I say access It, I'm speaking about all the Promises that God has given to us through Salvation in Jesus Christ that He has made available through the Knowledge of Him as it says in 2 Peter1:4. If we don't understand the dynamics of the Laws of the Spirit of Life that we have through Christ Jesus, then we're subject to the laws of sin and death as It says in Romans 8:2.

The Bible is full of Spiritual Laws and Principles that have to be applied in order to receive the manifestation of the Promises God has given to us in His Covenant. The Blood of Jesus Christ is absolutely VITAL to receive Them. His Blood was the Covenant Price that He paid in full for Salvation to be given to everyone who enters into this Covenant by being born again. The Blood is what redeems us and purges us through time in our journey here on Earth. It is what has made us holy and acceptable to God in the Beloved Jesus. (1 Peter 2:5). Almighty God accepted His Sacrifice of His Life as it states in Hebrews 10:10 and Verse 14. And because He did, He forever made us perfect by His Sacrifice once for all. Hebrews 10 tells us about what Jesus did for us because of the Cross He endured. God, seeing us now in Christ Jesus, sees us blameless, freeing us from sin conscience to righteousness, as we take the mind of Christ and become renewed in the spirit of our mind. We MUST see ourselves the same way! FREED! Freed from every curse of the law, now living by the Law of the Spirit in Christ Jesus! Look at the word 'sin' & 'curse' the same way. *Because they are the same thing*. Sins are what happen because of sin. When we see that sin IS the curse, then Grace comes in and takes It's rightful place in us through faith in Christ Jesus if we're born again. Now we can see ourselves freed from sin and all of the curse!

God shows us in Deuteronomy 28:15-68 what these curses include. Understand, there is a *causative* narration in the translations of the Bible. God doesn't put these upon us, we put them upon ourselves by following Satan and his demons be*CAUSE* we live in a fallen world. *God was warning us in Deuteronomy what will happen beCAUSE we* _aren't following Him!_ He knew what would happen to us be_CAUSE_ of the curse, so He's warning us what will be if we don't! Can you see it? Jesus, the Second Adam (man), came to give us life as The Word says in John 10:10 taking us out from what the curse had CAUSED because of the first Adam (man).

And when we do sin, we have an advocate, Jesus Christ, (1 John 2:1), as we confess our sins, He is faithful and just to forgive us of that sin. (1 John 1:9) It was His Blood that has redeemed us, overcoming every obstacle that Satan throws our way, and by the Word of our Testimony. (Rev. 12:11). This is now our Protection and the way to close every door that Satan would've had access to if we don't repent.

Of course, if we sin and don't ask for God to forgive us, then we've just opened ourselves to consequences in the natural, where Satan is god. (2 Cor. 4:4) We have to keep ourselves in Christ, being obedient to His Word through His Covenant, or give access to the natural. Many times, this is through our words being in agreement, or covenant, with Satan. This is the cause that comes, as I spoke of earlier, being human in a fallen world. This is how the Law of the Spirit of Life works in Christ Jesus that frees us from the law of sin and death. Romans 8:2. God is SO good! He thought of it all for us! Redemption through Jesus Christ! His Way is the way out of every circumstance and situation that comes against us in this World system. The Word System is The Way, The Truth & The New Life, and His Name is Jesus! John 1:1-14

14

The Power of Agreement

COVENANT MEANS AGREEMENT. When we speak the Word of God, we are agreeing with what His Word says about us. In Deuteronomy 30:19, God spoke about the power of life and death being set before us, Blessing and cursing. He then told us to choose life. Then Proverbs 18:21 says that the Power of life and death is in our tongue and that which we are inclined to will be the fruit that manifests in our lives. What this means is that we get to choose which Covenant we are in agreement with. Life; the Covenant of God's Blessing through Christ Jesus: death; the covenant of the curse with Satan. It's as simple as that. What we choose to speak and be in agreement with, will be that which will manifest in our lives. It's all done with our words and belief in them.

THE FOREVER WILL BE; *THE REVELATION OF MY NEW IDENTITY OF BEING*

The life that I now live, I live according to the Spirit being led by The Spirit. I live by the new law of The Spirit of Life in Christ Jesus. A new species of being that has never been before Jesus. Why?

God had put His Divine Seed in Adam and wanted a creation of this Species of Being, called mankind. The Seed corrupted when Satan stepped in and that generation stopped. When the Holy Ghost hovered over Mary, this Divine Seed was once again implanted into mankind. Now, when a person is 'born again', this Incorruptible Seed has totally over ridden the corruptible one. This is the new man that old things have passed away, all things are become new. This is the Spiritual Dynamic that has once again put into mankind again, only better. This one has been completed in Christ. He has come to live within us, through Holy Spirit, residing in us, growing us up into our new man identity. He is superseding every curse that courses through these earthly vessels, purging us, cleansing us of all unrighteousness, (the curse), and it's done in time. Some dynamics are quick, others are processed. Either way, we must continue to walk in the Truth of what has already happened to us within, every day, walking in faith expecting the Promises of God to manifest in us as we go through time. We become the, "as He is, so are we in this world." (1 John 4:17) In the world, but not of it. Renewed to the Word of God in our spirit man, our new, never been before species of being, led by the Spirit, not the flesh. Transformed from glory to glory. Trusting, believing in the Greater One Who lives in me. Romans 8:9-17. The Book of Romans is a Spiritual Eye opening Book as to who we now are in Christ Jesus. I encourage you to devour It. As a matter of fact, do the same with ALL of the Word of God, as we all know, we are what we eat!

15

Into The Promise

Daily Stepping Stones

Day 1 - The Line in the sand: making a qualified decision.

James 1:6-8 "But let him ask in faith, nothing wavering. For he that wavereth is like a wave of the sea driven with the wind and tossed. For let not that man think that he shall receive anything of the Lord. A double minded man is unstable in all his ways."

If you're going to get your healing, you're going to have to make a decision. Either you're going to hold fast to your decision of faith that you are already healed, or you're not. If you waver in the spirit of your mind, (your heart, your born again man), then it means that you won't be healed. This is one of the hardest things that you're going to have to do. But if you couldn't do it, then God wouldn't have told you that you could be healed. We can do all things through Christ as it says in Philippians 4:13. This is why it's so important to be renewed in the spirit of our mind by The Word of God. This will bring you to the reason of why Romans 8 verses 2 & 6 say what they do. You're living a new life in Christ now, if you're born again. You are now a spirit being, alive in Christ Jesus. (Galatians 2:20) To get what God says you can have, you've got to take a spiritual position of absolute resolve to believe The Word of God. The spirit realm is eternal. Everything in the physical realm is temporal. Disease is only physical and temporal. Healing is spiritual and eternal. The spirit realm trumps the physical realm. It's how God brought into the World and the Universe into physical reality. He spoke the Word. It's the same thing for us. It's going to be how you are going to be physically healed. Settle the matter, once for all. "I AM HEALED." *"Speak the Word only and my servant shall be healed..."* Matthew 8:8

Day 2 - Trusting with all your heart.

(AMPC) Proverbs 3:5-6; 5: Lean on, trust in, and be confident in the Lord with all your heart and mind and do not rely on your own insight or understanding. 6: In all your ways know, recognize, and acknowledge Him, and He will direct and make straight and plain your paths.

"Do you trust Me?" "Yes, Lord, I trust You."

"Now do you trust Me?" "Yes, Lord, I trust You."

"Do you trust Me now?" "Yes, Lord, I trust You now."

"If that what it takes for you to trust Me, is minute by minute, then that's what I need you to do."

This conversation went on between The Lord and I during a very dark time in my life. This lesson given to me through Holy Spirit never left me, especially when I received the diagnosis of 3rd stage lung cancer that had spread into the lymph nodes.

Battling in the mind when a doctor's report is negative, or a child that is wayward, or a debt that seems surmounting is not an easy thing to do. But with God and His Word of Promise, we can do all things through Christ! (Philippians 4:13)

During the journey through the wilderness, I heard the Lord speak to my spirit, "Don't let your hand go before My steps ordered." In Psalms 37:23, it says that the steps of a good man are ordered by the Lord. My righteousness and goodness lies completely in what Jesus Christ has done for me through Salvation. When I heard this about my hand going before my steps, I knew that He was saying that I needed to go back to the lesson learned years ago about trusting Him. I wasn't to get in the way with the "what ifs", "what about", or "what am I going to do about", all the how, what, where, when and why had to be totally left in the Hands of my Maker, my Healer, my Deliverer. Total trust, total surrender to Him.

Day 3 - My delay is not God's denial.

2 Corinthians 1:20: For all of God's promises have been fulfilled in Christ with a resounding "Yes!" And through Christ, our "Amen" (which means "Yes") ascends to God for his glory. NLT

God is a Covenant God and there is expectancy from both Him and us in order to receive His Promises to us. Another name for Covenant is agreement. He'll do His part if we'll do ours.

I had to get some things right in my life that I had foolishly been doing that God had been trying to get through to me, but I, not wanting to let go of my fleshly desires, kept putting Him off. God's Promises are yes to us, but there is a part that we, many times, have to put into order in our lives to receive His Healing. For me, that was food. I was blessing my food, but the food wasn't nutritious; no intake of water, diet pop, fried food, fast food, chips, candy, ice cream, desserts. "Bless this Lord and let it go to the good only of my body. Amen!" I don't think so. When the diagnosis came, so did the awakening.

We want the quick miraculous power to just take away the disease, but if the root of the problem isn't dealt with, then the disease will return. Jesus said to many of those that He healed, "Go and sin no more." This wasn't a suggestion. He knew what would happen if they did.

Don't wait to correct what you know that you need to do. Ask for God's Grace to empower you to do what you cannot do on your own. That's what He's there for. And then listen and obey. Then the "Yes and Amen", will be your declaration and your testimony of healing and deliverance!

Day 4 - Knowing God loves me.

Galatians 5:6 "For in Jesus Christ, neither circumcision availeth anything, nor uncircumcision; but faith which worketh by love."

I had read this verse so many times in the Bible. What I thought it meant was that my faith would work when I walked in love. But one day I was made aware of a different way of seeing this.

Faith which works by love is when we realize how much God really loves us. He gave us His only Son, Jesus Christ, to die on the Cross for us. To carry the weight of all of our sins, our diseases, our poverty, our death. Think about that for a moment. Let this Truth settle into your thought for a moment. Jesus, yes, the Son of God, leaving the Eternal realm of Glory, Light and Love and entering into this physical realm of death, disease and darkness in order to redeem us back to relationship and right standing with God, our Heavenly Father. God wanted His family back. He wanted relationship with us. He wanted us to know Him as our Father. He never intended for us to live under a curse. All He wanted to do was Bless us, His very own children, take care of us, provide for us, bring us life and health and love and prosperity. There isn't any sickness in Heaven; no disease; no poverty; no death. He wanted someone to love.

When we realize this Revelation of Truth of how much He loves us, then our faith in Him soars to the highest heights! We can trust and believe that He really does want to Bless us! He wants to heal us! He wants to prosper us! Our faith works when we know that we can trust Him and that He will never let anything harm us. It's the Great Exchange, our curse, His Blessing. This is how faith works by love.

Day 5 - The Revelation of "I AM"

Exodus 15:26 "And said, "If thou diligently hearken to the voice of the Lord thy God, and will do that which is right in his sight, and will give ear to his commandments, and keep all his statutes, I will put none of the diseases upon thee, which I brought upon the Egyptians: for I AM the Lord that healeth thee."

I AM is a Covenant name of God. It is Who He is, the same yesterday, today, and forever. He will never change. His Word and His Promise are One. He makes sure that what He has said, He will do. *(Isaiah 55:11)*

One day I was speaking out loud my confessions of God's Word. When I said, as it says in 1 Peter 2:24, "By his stripes *I AM* healed," suddenly I heard this differently. Instead of hearing that, "… by His stripes I am healed", I heard that "..by His Stripes *I AM* HEALED." He was revealing to me in my spirit that the Great I AM has done this for me! Not that, "I am healed", but that the Great I AM has healed me!

Now, let me go further. With The Covenant Name of *I AM*, whenever I say anything in The Word that begins with '*I AM*', what I"m speaking is God's Covenant, His Promise, over my life. "*I AM* delivered." "*I AM* whole." *I AM* redeemed." "*I AM* prosperous." The *I AM* always proceeds before the declaration. He goes before me. Hear what Deuteronomy 31:8 NIV says, *"The LORD himself goes before you and will be with you; he will never leave you nor forsake you. Do not be afraid; do not be discouraged."* Do you see it? What an Awesome God we serve!

These days when I introduce myself, I always say, *"I AM* Pamela Harding." His Covenant proceeds me, who I am, who He has said that I am, who He has created me to be. Totally confident that He's got this. He is The Great *I AM*.

Day 6 - Let go, let God.

> *Philippians 3:3 "Brethren, I count not myself to have appre-*
> *hended: but this one thing I do, forgetting those things which*
> *are behind, and reaching forth unto those things which are*
> *before,"*

My personality in the past has been to carry. Carry people's problems, to hold onto within, making sure that everyone is happy, at the cost of my own happiness. I became fearful whenever things would get out of order in my life. Smooth sailing. That's the kind of life I like. So when things were not going as I thought they should, I would worry within. Very anxious, taking hours to go to sleep because I was running through the course of the day and planning on how to fix it all tomorrow. Problem with this was that I wasn't ever supposed to do this.

Because of these tendencies, I started having panic attacks. And because I would focus on them, afraid of them happening, I had no idea that I was bringing them on. What was once just a couple of times a day began to happen more frequently. Soon, every waking moment of my day was filled with them. It was horrible. The only relief I would get was when I finally would fall asleep, exhausted from the mental torment.

One day, my oldest sister came to see me. She said something that was so simple, yet so profound. "Let go and let God." Sadly, in the state that I was in, I had to truly seek Him to find out what this meant. Let go? You mean, I don't have to carry this? I don't have to feel like this? I can just completely quit worrying about everything? When this Truth finally made It's way within my spirit, because I meditated on this alone, the healing began. The attacks became less and less because I no longer was focused on them. I focused on The Lord and His Promise of healing for me. Giving me His Love, His Life, His Joy, His Peace. I could really just let go and enter into His Rest.

Enter in. Let go and let God. He's really good at taking all our problems, making them His Own. And giving us His Blessing of healing; the Ultimate Health Care Package.

Day 7 - "Yes, My Grace provided it..."

Ephesians 2:8 "For by grace are ye saved, through faith; and that not of yourselves: it is the gift of God:"

In one portion of my book, Out of The Wilderness, I told of a time when I had been ministering to someone who was a Christian, that I had known for a long time, who had cancer and hospice had just come in to her home.

She passed several months later, and when I found out, I had an internal discussion with myself. Turned out that it was God that I was discussing this matter with.

Because I had been healed from cancer, when I found out that my friend had died, I said within, "But by the grace of God go I." Suddenly, from deep within me, I heard a resounding, *"NO! Yes My Grace provided it, but you had to take it!"* It jolted me, realizing that God was saying something to me very profound.

Salvation came through God's Grace. In the Greek, salvation is the word 'soteria'; the definition is deliverance, preservation, safety. God was telling me that His Grace was the reason for my salvation, but in order to receive the manifestations of His Blessing of redemption from the curse of disease, I had to take it by faith. My laying down with the disease wasn't going to attain my healing. Matthew 11:12b says that the Kingdom of Heaven suffers violence, and the violent take it by force.

Everything has to be received by us, salvation, healing, deliverance, and prosperity. It's not going to just 'fall on us', we've got to take it through faith. And we've got an enemy that is out to steal, kill & destroy us. (John 10:10) God's Word has the Power in Itself to bring Itself to pass. But if you're not following the Word of God in obedience to what He has shown us through His Word, by speaking His Word, agreeing with His Word, and establishing His Word in our lives through faith, then even though It has the Power, it won't produce anything for us. The Word works, but we've got to work the Word. And once you've taken it, don't let go of it until it happens in your life.

Day 8 - The thing you think the longest is the strongest.

1 Timothy 4:15 "Meditate upon these things; give thyself wholly to them; that thy profiting may appear to all."

This revelation of what we give most thought to will determine the strength of that thing in our lives, was given to me when I was having anxiety attacks. What I was focusing on in my mind gave place to that being created in my reality.

We are created in the image of God. (Genesis 1:26-27) Therefore, we have the ability to be creative. It's in our minds that the creative gifts and talents that we have flow. As we build it up in our mind, we see it, we then have the ability to create that in the natural realm. Whether it's a poem, a piece of art, a craft, all of these began as a thought in our mind. This is our inner man. He has all five senses that our outward natural man has; touch, taste, sight, hearing, smelling. (2 Corinthians 6:17, Psalms 34:8, Isaiah 6:10, 2 Corinthians 2:15)

It is no difference in what we create in the areas of either health or sickness, life or death. James 4:7 tells us to submit to God and resist the devil. One of the Greek definitions of devil here is *malicious statements*. Words. Words are seeds, and if a seed is planted it will produce after its own kind. (Luke 8:11, Genesis 1:11-12)

Genesis 2:7 says that we are made out of dirt. What happens when you plant a seed in dirt? *It will produce after its kind.* The creative power we have within, whatever we give place to, the Doctors report or The Report of the Lord, will be the very thing that will be produced in our lives. This is why The Word of God tells us to *be renewed in the spirit of our mind.* (Ephesians 4:23)

Romans 12:2 says that if we'll be renewed in our minds, this will transform our lives, proving The Word of God and what His Will is for us in this world. Think on The Word of God. It will transform your lives into His Promises.

Day 9 - Every lie of the enemy was a brick to my foundation.

Ephesians 6:16 "Above all, taking the shield of faith, wherewith ye shall be able to quench all the fiery darts of the wicked."

I'm so thankful for all of The Word of God that had been poured into my life. Whether by Holy Spirit, a Preacher, a Teacher, a friend, my own study. When push comes to shove, this is when you realize how much of The Word is alive and active in our lives.

Years ago, while going through a very difficult time, the enemy of my soul was wreaking havoc in my mind. I had so much inner self talk of my own going on that was negative, to have more lies being thrown at me was more than I could handle. I cried out to the Lord and He heard me....

In an open vision, I remembered the Scripture in Ephesians 6 that tells us to put on The Armor of God. As I saw myself holding The Shield of Faith, I saw a brick thrown at it. I saw it fall below me. Another brick was thrown and fell down at my feet. These were lies that were being spoken within my soul. Lies of doubt, fear, dread of what was happening to me and all around me. As I took another glance below, I saw these bricks were being laid under my feet. They were forming a solid foundation that I was able to stand on, because I was casting them down with The Shield by my faith. And with every brick thrown, I was rising up with them. Rising above the lies. Rising above the fear. Rising above the enemy.

Many times we don't understand what is going on in the Spirit realm because we're too focused on the natural. Yes, I was getting stuff thrown at me left and right, but because I saw things in a different light and perspective, these things were no longer taking me down because I was overtaking them by faith.

> *Psalms 91:13; "Thou shalt tread upon the lion and the adder: the young lion and the dragon shalt thou trample under foot."*

Day 10 - "You speak it, I'll do it."

Isaiah 46:10a "Declaring the end from the beginning,"

There were many days that I battled in my mind. The memories of past experiences of cancer through other people's lives would plague me. Going daily to treatments and seeing the results of cancer in the bodies of those who were also taking treatment didn't help the thoughts going through my head. I had to fight those images I saw, those internal words of doubt trying to be louder than The Word of God's Promises to me.

One morning while meditating and reading The Bible, I heard within, *"You speak it, I'll do it."* Now I had already been declaring the Word over my life and was adamant about keeping the words that I spoke in line with what God said. I knew the Power of Covenant, whether in life with Jesus, or death with satan, so I guarded what came out of my mouth. No complaining. No doubts. No reasoning. No planning on doing anything but living. I was not going to allow my flesh to get in the way of my healing. No matter what I was feeling or thinking.

I would imagine myself healthy. Riding my bicycle again. Running. Never did like running, but I would see myself running anyway! Even this would spark something within, causing me to laugh at myself running. Proverbs 17:22 says, "A merry heart doeth good like a medicine: but a broken spirit drieth the bones." So whatever would bring laughter, I went for it. Old movies, funny moments in my life, funny videos; anything that would bring me joy, I filled myself with.

No, this wasn't easy. But it was necessary. I knew what God's Word said that I had to do, so I did it. There were days that I would cry out asking God to help any unbelief in me. I said many times, "His strength is made perfect in my weakness." The course of time proved what God had spoken to my heart.

"If you shall ask anything in My Name, I will do it." John 14:14

Day 11 - Praying over everything...

> Revelation 12:11 *"And they overcame him by the blood of the Lamb, and the word of their testimony; and they loved not their lives unto the death."*

During this time of my life, because of our insurance through my job, I had to take wellness exams in order to keep up my insurance requirements.

I had made an appointment to have a routine mammogram done. While waiting with my gown on for the technician, I saw an open vision in the room. I saw a demon go up to the machine where my breast would lay, and put his grimy hand on the plate. The vision continued on as I saw this play out in another person's life. The results showed something was seen on the x-rays of the breast. When they got the call, fear immediately gripped them. This opened the door for the devil to begin the destruction of this woman's life. Suddenly it was over.

The Lord had already given me a strategy of what I was to do when I decided to take the radiation and chemo treatments. He told me that I wasn't to allow anything into my body without praying over it and Blessing it to the good of my body first. Any equipment that would be touching my body, I was to do the same thing and declare the results to be normal. Blood tests, radiation machines, blood pressures, thermometers, you name it, I prayed over them first.

It was later that I had the open vision and I understood then why I was to cover everything with the Blood of Jesus. My prayers were, and still are, "In The Name of Jesus, satan, you'll not touch, alter, afflict or change any of these reports from being anything but The Report of The Lord. I cover all these tests and results with The Blood of The Lamb."

We don't have full understanding of the Realm of the Spirit in this Earth realm, but believe me, demons are real and every opportunity that they can take, they will, but only if we let them.

> *"The thief cometh not, but for to steal, and to kill, and to destroy: I am come that they might have life, and that they have it more abundantly." John 10:10*

Day 12 - "There is no battle that you will go into that I have not destined for you to win."

2 Chronicles 20:15b "Thus saith the Lord unto you, Be not

afraid nor dismayed by reason of this great multitude; for the battle is not yours, but God's."

Now, this can get confusing. I've stated already that the battle is in the mind, but this Scripture says that the battle is God's. Let me give you some understanding of this verse.

When we became born again, we were translated, or moved into the Kingdom of God out of the kingdom of darkness. (Colossians 1:13) Satan no longer has any power over us. The only power that he has is what we give him through our agreement with him. Agreement with him is through the physical realm we're still in and this by our words and thoughts. This is why the power of life and death are in the tongue. (Proverbs 18:21) And why we have to submit to God, resist the devil and he has to flee. (James 4:7) This is completely done by faith, because the Kingdom of God has spiritual laws and the Law of Faith is how it is governed by. (Romans 3:27-28)

Jesus has completely defeated him. (Colossians 2:15) And He's turned this Authority and rule over to us. (Luke 10:19) This is why the battle was God's in the Old Testament, because Jesus hadn't defeated satan yet. But now, he's done for. And this is why there isn't a battle that we go through in this physical realm that God hasn't destined and determined for us to completely win.

The only access satan has is through our thoughts and words. And that, only if you rent him space in your mind.

Day 13 - I refuse to be moved....

Ephesians 6:13-14 "Wherefore take unto you the whole armour of God, that you me be able to withstand in the evil day, and having done all, to stand. Stand therefore,..."

This very day that I'm writing this devotional has been a very, very

---

trying day. You see, there are still things that I believe God to heal in this physical body. Other diagnoses were given before the cancer and I just did nothing to resist it. Take a couple of pills, yeah, I'm healed, but I wasn't fighting the good fight of faith. I called that sleeping with the giants. (Numbers 33:55) These giants were taking over this physical and I just let them.

With that being said, these diseases were allowed to exist and therefore, they took ground, so to speak. Many times, when diseases have been allowed by us without resistance, it's like a weed that has been allowed to keep growing without anything stopping it's development. The roots get deeper and stronger. So, this fight of faith has been a bit harder.

Yes, Jesus Christ has already healed me. Even when the symptoms are screaming louder than The Scriptures, louder than what my mind is racing around with, it doesn't matter. The Truth trumps the facts. I AM HEALED. This is what Ephesians is speaking about...*stand.* In the Greek, it means stay in the place that you've been given. God has given me health and wholeness in Jesus Christ because of His sacrifice on the cross. The Word of God also says that my life is hidden with Christ in God. (Colossians 3:3) This is where I take my stand, with Christ. This is the place that I have been given. So I'm not moved by what I feel. I walk by faith, not by what I'm feeling.

> *"If you're willing to stand forever, you won't be there long."*
> Kenneth Hagin

Day 14 - *What are you considering?*

> Romans 4:19 *"And not being weak in faith, he considered not his own body now dead, when he was about an hundred years old, neither yet the deadness of Sara's womb:"*

Consider not, consider not, consider not. These words are still resounding within me. Consider not? Don't think about? The Strongs definition of consider is to fix one's eye's or mind upon. When I had been given all the different diagnoses, I had a choice to make. I had to choose what I thought about. Still have to do this today. I have a choice to make every day that I wake up, whose report am I going to believe? Joshua 24:15 tells us that we have to choose who we're going to serve. The god's that our father's served, disease, generational curses in the lineage of sickness of our ancestors or The Lord? What and who am I going to listen to? Who am I going to fix my mind upon? What am I going to look at?

We are internally ruled. It's just a fact. Our direction of perception will become our conception. Did you get that? What we continue to focus on will be what will be birthed in our lives. I had to and still have to see myself completely healed. I see myself running. I see myself riding my bike up hills without having to stop to catch my breath. I see myself without pain. I see The Lord upon the cross with every one of my diseases and malformations upon His Body. I have to make myself see this.

This doesn't come easy. One has to take the time to meditate on it. Even in the midst of pain. In the midst of the diseased parts. In the midst of it all. I have and you have to consider health. Consider wholeness. Fully persuaded of God. *Consider not your own body*....

Romans 4:21 "And being fully persuaded that, what he had promised, he was able also to perform"

Day 15 - Turning inward on myself

1 Peter 5:7 "Casting all your care upon him; for he careth for you.

I heard this not too long ago. That one cannot turn the matters inward upon themselves. When I heard this, it captivated me for a moment.

This spoke to me, because that is the type of person that I've been.

I've always been a bit of a loner, by choice. I am comfortable with myself, never had to have a bunch of people around me, able to sit quietly alone. No noise, no outside stimulus, just me and my thoughts. As wonderful as this can be for me, it can also be my downfall.

Reflecting upon turning things inward on myself, I had a tendency to be in this mode of self-checking. Am I saying The Word enough? Am I praying enough? Am I spending time alone with God enough? Then I would become condemned over it because the answer, for the most part, was no. I would then allow these tormenting thoughts begin to cascade my mind with doubt and anxiety as to whether God's going to heal me because *I've not been good enough.*

The Word of God says that He's my Healer. He's the One that will do it. Not because of my works, but *because of His.* The age old question, "Hath God said, " would begin the check list inwardly.

I had to again, make a decision to throw that check list out. Not to pick it back up. Not to go over it again in my mind, not to turn the care inwardly upon myself, but to cast it. Let go. Let God. He said it, I believe it. And that has to settle it.

Day 17 - I am my own prophet

> Job 22:28 "Thou shalt also decree a thing, and it shall be established unto thee: and the light shall shine upon they ways.

When one realizes the power that our mouths have over ourselves, it makes you stop and think. What you are living today is what you have spoken in the past.

God's Word is full of Scriptures concerning the power of our tongue. We've been created in His Image. When God first began all of

---

Creation, it all started because He spoke. And if we're created as He is, then everything we speak will be that which we will live.

This is a Spiritual Law that God set in motion at the beginning of time. We live in a word activated system. And we either will live by every word we speak or die by them. We cannot mix our speech. We have to line our words up with God's Word. This cannot be said enough.

Thank God for His Grace because if we ever came to the place where what we said would happen immediately, most people would be dead. All one has to do is tune their ears to what is being spoken and pay attention to what is being said, we'd then have a greater understanding of where their words and lives are matching up.

You cannot talk about your disease. Your pain. Your fears. If you are, then you cannot expect anything of God.

James 1:6-8 But let him ask in faith, nothing wavering. For he that wavereth is like a wave of the sea driven with the wind and tossed. For let not that man think that he shall receive any thing of the Lord. A double minded man is unstable in all his ways.

Pretty plain isn't it?

Day 18 - "I already did this for you..."

Galatians 3:13 "Christ hath redeemed us from the curse of the law, being made a curse for us: for it is written, Cursed is every one that hangeth on a tree:"

The very first day that I had to go in for chemo and radiation treatments, I was nervous, but still had peace within. I didn't know what I was going into because I hadn't taken the classes that the hospital wanted me to take to learn about "my cancer". I refused to make it mine, nor allow anyone around me to put that on me.

As I went into the radiation room, I did as The Lord directed me to lay my hands on the machine, pray out loud declaring my healing in Jesus Name. As instructed, I laid down on the long bed that would then slide me into the tube. Just as I did, I went into an open vision:

Jesus came and laid right down on top of me, facing the same direction as I was, looking upward, and His Body totally engulfed mine. He then turned His Head to the side, looking down toward me and said, "I've already done this for you." And just as quick as He was there, He was gone.

The anxiety completely left me. How could it stay? I had been in the Presence of My Healer. The Truth of His Word was coming to pass in my life. All I had to do was believe.

This is all that The Lord asks of us, only believe...

> Romans 10:9 "That if thou shalt confess with thy mouth the Lord Jesus, and shalt believe in thine heart that God hath raised him from the dead, thou shalt be saved."

Day 19 - "Do not be so impressed by what you feel that you forget Who you know."

> Psalms 91:2 "I will say of the LORD, He is my refuge and my fortress: my God; in him will I trust."

When I was going through anxiety and panic attacks, there wasn't any time in over 3 years that I had peace while I was awake. I was seeking God to give me peace, help me to find my way through this wilderness that was wreaking havoc in my life.

One Sunday afternoon, our house was filled with people and I was watching a t.v. program. The room was loud and I was aggravated because I would do anything I could to try to focus on something other than the fear I was feeling within.

Suddenly, it was as if the Red Sea parted in front of me. A clearing was made before me, allowing me to both hear and see the television. This is what I heard: "Don't be so impressed by what you feel that you forget what you know." Feeling. He just talked about feeling. Not to think more about that than any truth that I knew. That I could give Truth a greater place within me than the place of fear that was ruling me because of what I was feeling.

That was over 25 years ago. I still teach and use this valuable word that came to me in the midst of a very great storm that was going on in my life. I've used this over and over as a tool for guidance personally. Anything that tries to be greater than my Lord Jesus Christ is a lie. And that's the Truth!

Day 20 - "The giants you've defeated are the ones who have retreated."

Numbers 33:55: "But if ye will not drive out the inhabitants of the land from before you; then it shall come to pass, that those which ye let remain of them shall be pricks in your eyes, and thorns in your sides, and shall vex you in the land wherein ye dwell."

Talk about a wakeup call! When I originally was diagnosed with several diseases before the cancer diagnosis, I knew what I needed to do, speak The Word of God, meditate on The Scriptures of healing, spending time getting them into my heart. But I chose not to. Yes, I knew that the Word said I was healed, so I just went on with my daily life, taking the meds that I had been prescribed and just living with it. When the diagnosis of cancer came, I knew that I wasn't going to be living with anything long if I didn't get serious about pursuing The Promises of God. Not long after, I was listening to a teacher of The Word; he quoted this Verse in Numbers and my Spirit shook me. It shook me awake, is what it did. If I continued as I was, then it was going to be the end of my life as I knew it on Earth.

Daily I began searching all The Scriptures on healing, meditating on Them, speaking Them out loud, several times a day, focusing on Them until They truly were now written on the tablets of my heart. After some time, I _knew_ I was healed before I ever got the all clear from the doctors.

The cancer after 6 months was gone, the rheumatoid arthritis was gone about 6 months later, along with several other auto immune diseases that had been diagnosed.

The choice is ours. Jesus said in John 19:30, "It is finished." And it was, on His Part, now we've got to do our part, working out our Salvation and receiving it by faith through The Word of God.

Day 21 - "Speak the word only..."

Matthew 8:8; "The centurion answered and said, Lord, I am not worthy that thou shouldest come under my roof: but speak the word only, and my servant shall be healed."

This Scripture is so powerful! Speak the word only, speak the word only....

I know that I've alluded to this on a previous day, but I can't stress this enough, _you can't just think about the Word, you've got to speak It!_

The centurion in the Scripture understood authority. He was a high ranking soldier in the Roman Army. He knew what it meant to obey a command when one of those who were over him said it, then he had to do it! And he knew this about Jesus. All He had to do was speak The Word and his servant would be healed!

Satan is the author of disease, not God. It's part of the curse that Jesus has redeemed us from. And Jesus, took all authority away from Satan and has given us the victory over all the schemes of the enemy, so that nothing shall harm us.

Jesus IS The Word. You cannot separate Him from The Word. And He IS all Authority. These are Spiritual Truths that if you will take hold of them, meditate on Them, then They will take hold of you! You will understand when you speak, Jesus IS speaking through you. When you command the disease to leave and for your body to be healed in Jesus Name, Jesus IS speaking through you with all Authority over satan and disease. When **_you_** know this, so does satan and the disease, then, through your faith, your healing then comes.

> *Luke 10:19 "Behold I give unto you power to tread on serpents and scorpions, and over all the power of the enemy: and nothing shall by any means hurt you."*

Day 22 - "And the Lord answered me, and said, Write the vision, and make it plain upon tables, that he may run that readeth it." Habakkuk 2:2

Television: tell a vision. Who creates the programming? **_The producers._**

Because we are created in the image of God, (Genesis 1:27), throughout The Word of God, it is written over and over that we are to keep God's Word before our eyes, speaking it into the hearing of our own ears.

Our minds are creative. It's where the imagination is and where creativity flows. Our eyes and ears are gates that allow things to effect what our imaginations can produce. Television is a huge obstacle in the lives of people today.

Satan cannot tempt us with what we do not know. Much of the information that we allow to enter into these gates come through television. These days, programs and commercials are filled with fear, disease, symptoms, medications, lawyers wanting victims, all of which have to do with illness and death, not health and wholeness. By our allowance of these things coming into our 'gates', our eyes and ears, they begin to cause us to reflect upon them. Thinking about them brings us to worry and fear, which are both *producers* of these things that we're imagining. We connect them to possible symptoms, diseases, family members, friends who've related those things to us. They begin to 'tell a vision' to our souls, which produces that which we are allowing. Ephesians 4:27 says, "Neither give place to the devil." One of the Greek definitions of the word devil means, 'malicious statements'. Words. We live in a word activated Earth, it's how God called it into being, all of it through words. Satan knows this, but doesn't want us to know this.

Don't allow your gates to tell a vision of death, disease, fear, anxiety and worry. Keep the Word of God before your eyes and in your ears, for, "they are life to those that find them, and health to all their flesh...." Proverbs 4:22

Day 23 - "Making the word of God of none effect through your tradition, which ye have delivered: and many such like things do ye." Mark 7:13

Is it possible that we have made God's Power ineffectual in our lives because we are not taking The Word of God and The Gospel literally?

The Gospel means "too good to be true news". If we've allowed man's traditions and religious doctrine to infiltrate the literal Word of God, then there is no power left in it.

We've made it 'relatable' to man. We've made The Word conform to us instead of us conforming to The Word. If It's written in The Bible, and someone comes and preaches another way of looking at it, other than what it says, then we've taken that very Word, which Jesus said in John 6:63, *"It is the spirit that quickeneth; the flesh profiteth nothing: the words that I speak unto you, they are spirit and they are life.",* and have moved it from the Spirit realm into the format of the doctrine of demons. *"But though we, or an angel from heaven, preach any other gospel unto you that than which we have preached unto you, let him be accursed."* Galatians 1:8

So His Word is what produces life giving Power! Quickeneth means to make one alive! If anything preached or taught is in anyway contrary to The Word of God, then it is of no effect. No life giving power to our spirit or our flesh.

Take the Word of God literally. When you read The Bible, look at it through new eyes. Ask Holy Spirit for The Truth of The Word. What did It mean? How do I make it applicable in my own, personal life today. After all, only The Word of God produces life, this flesh cannot do anything for us. If it could, then there would be no need for a Savior.

Day 24 - *"He sent his word, and healed them, and delivered them from their destructions." Psalms 107:20*

The Ultimate Health Care Package

Think about this: everything that we've ever done in our lives that could destroy us, Jesus Christ has delivered us from them all.

There is nothing left out. Absolutely nothing that you or I have done in the past can stand in the way of His Healing, Delivering Power to bring us out of the effects of those bad choices that we've made in our lives. This is The Gospel! The too good to be true news of Jesus Christ and His Resurrection Power that has redeemed us from the curse.

Our Salvation is the Power and the seal of Holy Spirit, through faith, to bring us through every situation that we, because of our bad choices, or the enemy of our souls, the devil, uses to destroy us. And that being done in the here and now!

> 2 Peter 1:3; "According as his divine power **hath** given unto us, all things that pertain unto life and godliness, through the knowledge of him that hath called us to glory and virtue."

Hath is past tense. Already done. That's what Jesus meant when on The Cross, He said it was finished! How do we attain this? Through the knowledge of him. Jesus Christ. His finished work. Salvation is our life eternal, health and prosperity in every avenue of life, here on Earth and in Heaven. Deuteronomy 11:21 speaks of our days as being, "... Heaven on Earth...". There is no sickness, no disease, no death, no poverty in Heaven. This is His Covenant that God made with His Son, Jesus Christ, and when we accepted Him as our Lord and Savior, this Promise was given to us and to our seed. But only accessed by the knowledge of Him and through faith, which you already have. If you've been born again, you already have enough faith to move any mountain in this life that stands in your way of The Promises' of God. But it works through knowing Him personally and by faith.

Take it, it's yours!

Day 25 - Mark 11:24 "Therefore I say unto you, What things soever ye desire, when you pray, believe that you receive them, and ye shall have them."

Okay, we're getting down to the nitty gritty here in these last pages of devotion. And the need for toppling over many sacred cows of false teachings and doctrines that have been taught which have made The Word of God of no effect.

We've gotten on the wrong track when we allow any experience that someone has had that is contrary to what The Word of God says, be our direction.

Poverty, sickness and disease are of the curse. Period. These are not used to teach anyone of us about God. He doesn't use them to teach us lessons. These are not 'blessings' that we must endure so that we can glorify God in our suffering. Where in The Word does it say that? When we believe the lie, The Truth of The Word cannot and will not prevail. How you believe, you shall receive.

Believe that any sickness or poverty is a 'blessing' from God and guess what, you shall have them....according to how you believe you shall receive! It's right there in The Word. It doesn't just say about the good things, it's referring to everything! Right, wrong or otherwise. Vine's dictionary speaks of that word desire in Mark 11:24 to mean what you call for. As you believe in your heart, so are you....

We have to take what The Word of God says as Truth. Not adding to it, or taking from it. Opinions have no place. Experience has no place. Disease has no place. Satan has no place. Render to God what belongs to Him. Sovereignty. Top billing. Top priority. Above all. For He alone is The Way, The Truth, and The Life.

Day 26 - John 3:8 "The wind blows (breathes) where it wills; and though you hear it's sound, yet you neither know where it comes from nor where it is going. So it is with everyone who is born of the Spirit." AMPC

I recently read a book that talked about faith. How that as perfume is to the senses, so is faith to the human spirit. We don't see it, yet it's presence is unmistakable.

As a child, I believed in Santa Claus. Only seeing him on t.v., or at a mall, I totally expected that this round, fat bodied man was going to make his way into my home and leave me all kinds of presents at

Christmas. Didn't understand how he was going to do it, but I left those details to him. I just believed.

When we were born again, even though we couldn't see it, faith was deposited into the very depth of our new spirit man within. The very faith of God implanted. The same faith that created the Universe and all of mankind was now present in me. And I could take anything that God had said in The Bible with that same faith and watch it come to pass.

Just as a child at Christmas, we must believe that He is and the Rewarder of those that diligently seek Him. (Hebrews 11:6) The Word says that we must be like a child to receive the Kingdom of God. Why? A child innocently rests on what he is told. No worries. No doubt. It was said, so it will be.

When we first begin to believe that we're healed, our natural, physical bodies, many times are saying otherwise. We don't feel it. There's no evidence of this being truth. Even so, we cannot doubt in our heart that we're not healed. We have to believe first, and then we see the result of our believing.

Our Heavenly Father desires us to fully trust in what He has Promised. He puts His Word above His Name. (Psalms 138:2) That's how much we can simply believe.

Day 27 - Philippians 4:13 "I can do all things through Christ which strengtheneth me."

> Jude 1:20 "But ye, beloved, building up yourselves on your most holy faith, praying in the Holy Ghost,"

In my own walk, there were days when my circumstances were louder than the Word of God in my spirit. In those moments, I had a choice to make. Am I going to succumb to what I am feeling, or am

I going hang on to what God's Word says, that "...*by His Stripes you were healed.*"

God has given man free will to make choices. We made the choice to accept Jesus as our Savior. Once we've done that, He wants to take the reins of our life. Notice that I said, He _wants_ to. Doesn't mean that He's going to force us to, He leaves that choice to us.

On those days when my body is being wracked with pain, or anything that is contrary to life and health, I have to make a choice as to who am I going to believe.

This is when I rise up in faith, take the Word of God and begin to speak It out loud to my body. I tell my body what it's to do. I speak peace to the storm that is going on in my mind. I praise, I sing, I decree The Word. I have the Gift of Tongues, so then I pray in The Holy Ghost, which truly does build up my faith, _my most holy faith!_

God's Word is Spirit and Life, (John 6:63), so when I begin to talk to myself, I am bringing Life to myself, to my spirit man, who I really am. I begin to take hold of The Word and I begin to feel exuberance within. I take back what the circumstances are trying to steal from me. I begin to soar again in faith, knowing that what my Father has said, He will do.

Day 28 - Matthew 6:31a "Therefore take no thought, saying...."

James 4:7 "Submit yourselves therefore to God. Resist the devil, and he will flee from you.

Genesis 1:27 "So God created man in his own image, in the image of God created he him, male and female created he them."

The Power of our Mind

When I had been diagnosed with cancer, every horrific, imaginable thought came across my mind. My funeral, my last days on Earth, who was going to be there, what would be said, what my diseased body was going to look and smell like, you name it, it came. Like a tsunami, my thoughts tried to rule over what The Word of God had said I could have.

The above Scriptures are so powerful. As you've been reading throughout this book, I have spoken over and over about the words that we speak, the things that we think, and that we have to make choices.

This, my dear reader, is where the power of the mind comes in. Because we've been created in the Image of God, we, too, have the very same creative power within us, for either death or life, blessing or cursing. God was trying to get us to understand those Truths' throughout His Word, telling us over and over, giving us the direction of what we need to do in order to have the life abundant that Jesus Christ died for us to have. He's given us the tools, they are the renewal of our minds by The Word of God, and faith to believe that what He has said, He will do.

While being in ministry, I cannot tell you how many times I've given these tools to Christians, who have been in Church most of their lives, and then have had to go to their funerals. I would tell them, "Don't be planning your funeral." "Don't be taking out life insurance now." Because where your mind goes, your body will truly follow. This is the creative power that we've been made in. These choices really are ours to make. God, in all of His Great Sovereignty, cannot and will not overstep our choices, which are our wills.

You and I have a daily choice to make, life or death, blessing or cursing. You choose, and whatever you choose, God will either permit, or step in to what we're believing for.

Day 29 - Matthew 6:31a "Therefore take no thought, saying...."

> James 4:7 "Submit yourselves therefore to God. Resist the devil, and he will flee from you.

> Genesis 1:27 "So God created man in his own image, in the image of God created he him, male and female created he them."

As I said in day 28, God has given us great power within us. It's in the soul. This isn't your brain, this is where your emotions, your will and your mind that chooses to either accept whatever flies into it, or rejects it.

When those thoughts of a funeral, death, disease, peoples' reactions, we've got a screen in our mind that plays out whatever we allow. None of these are just happenstance, they are whatever we've allowed in throughout our lives. As I've said previously, Satan cannot tempt you with what you do not know.

They tried to get me to learn about 'my cancer', take classes on what I would be going through, what emotions would take place during this time in my life, how my body was going to react and how to prepare for the end. Phhhtttt! No way! I hightailed it out of there. I thank God that I knew that I had a choice to make. Either I was going to take the highway of health and wholeness, or death. This battle of faith was what I had entered into. And this all goes on within the mind of every person. God said I was peculiar and this choice to not join this party proved it. I had a Covenant with God through Christ Jesus, and He had already done this great work of healing and health in me, and time was going to show Himself Strong on my behalf. The other behalf, my mind, was my part to play out.

The thing you think the longest is strongest. 2 Corinthians 10:5 "Casting down imaginations, and every high thing that exalteth itself *against the knowledge of God, and bringing into captivity every thought to the obedience of Christ;"*

Every thought, which are made up of words, I had to take inventory of. I had to think about what I was thinking about. And if it didn't line up with God's Promises, I had to stop, hit the eject button, throw it out, put in another visual, of healthy, whole Promises of life and blessing. AND SAY IT OUTLOUD. Over and over I had to do this. It wasn't easy, but, God wouldn't tell us to do something if He hasn't empowered us to do this.

> *Philippians 4:13 "I can do all things through Christ which strengthenth me."*

Day 30 - Philippians 1:28 "And in nothing terrified by your adversaries: which is to them an evident token of perdition, but to you of salvation, and that of God."

This Scripture is so powerful! This is the way that God is going to give you the Victory, if you obey it. Read that again. *"And in nothing terrified by your adversaries:…"* Nothing means nothing. No Doctors' report, no syptoms, no experiences of your family or friends, no commercials, nothing. The adversary is anything that says that you're going to die, your Mamma had this, your Daddy had this, that program you watched, they had it, your not healed, look at you, feel that? Everything will come at you from the adversary. Do not be terrified by them…in nothing.

"…which is to them an evident token of perdition," When you show no fear, then you've not fallen into their trap. Fear is a trap of Satan and if he can get you to be afraid, then he will win. It's either faith or fear. It's that black and white. No in between. When you stand, even in the midst of being afraid, and declare what God says only, this is PROOF to them that their end of their assignment against you is eminent.

"but to you of salvation, and that of God." Salvation was what you received when you accepted Jesus Christ as your Lord and Savior. If you've not already done this, there is a prayer at the very end of this devotional for you to pray. But for those of you who already are born again, the whole health and welfare package was given to you on that day of your new birth in Christ. Wholeness, health, soundness, prosperity, a blessed life here on Earth and Eternal life was given to you right at that very moment. Now believe it. God said it, Jesus said it was finished, so this work is complete. Now you've got to accept it. Get rid of all doubt. Get rid of all fear. Step into faith. Step into life. Step into Christ. It's all up to you. Choose Him.

If you've never accepted Jesus Christ as your Lord and Savior, and want to move out of the god of this world, Satan's rule over your life, then just open up your heart right now to receive Him. It's a Spiritual Truth that your natural mind will not be able to understand, but once you've done this, really done this, you will never be the same again.

Read the following out loud: *Jesus, I believe that You are The Son of Almighty God and that you came to Earth to bring us back to life and a relationship with our Heavenly Father. I believe that you died for me, took all of my sin and shame, nailed it to Your Cross, and have given me Your Righteousness in its place.*

Forgive me Jesus, for all that I've done, come into my heart and live. Change me, make me whole, heal my life, and do for me what I cannot do for myself. Wash me in Your Perfect Blood, making me white as snow, clean, free from all that held me bound. I receive you as my Lord and Savior for the rest of my life, here and for Eternity. In Jesus Name, Amen.

Welcome to the family dear one. The Angels are celebrating you right now. Your name has been written in The Lambs Book of Life and you have been given the right to run into The Throne room of Almighty God, Who now is your Heavenly Father. Never run from Him, run to Him. All that He has for you is good. He sees you completely clean, free from all sin. Find a Gospel Church, which allows The Holy Spirit free reign there, and grow up now, Spiritually, into the destiny that God has for you to live.

God Bless you, and if I never see you on this side of Heaven, I'll see you there for all of Eternity. Who knows, you might be my neighbor....

Pastor Pamela Harding

CPSIA information can be obtained
at www.ICGtesting.com
Printed in the USA
FFHW020956230919
55155394-60870FF

9 781977 2172